FOREWORD

One of the many joys of gardening is watching a seed sprout and grow into a plant. This seems like magic to a child, especially if they have heard the fairy tale, "Jack and the Beanstalk"!

The Saved Seed shows the young child that seeds originally come from nature. The seed saved from carving a pumpkin at Halloween guides the child through the year with all the basic steps in gardening that allows it to grow into a vine with new pumpkins for the next Halloween.

Gertrude Jekyll said, "The love of gardening is a seed once sown that never dies." Experience the wonder of nature with a child by saving and planting a seed, nurturing it and watching it grow. Share their joy, excitement and sense of accomplishment in the miracle of growing.

Garden clubs can be a resource for gardening with youth. Please visit the website of National Garden Clubs, Inc., www.gardenclub.org, for project ideas.

Nancy L. Hargroves
President 2017-2019
National Garden Clubs, Inc.

Printed in the United States of America

First Printing, 2017

ISBN 978-0-941994-21-7

National Garden Clubs, Inc.
4401 Magnolia Ave.
St. Louis, MO 63110

ph: 314-776-7574

www.gardenclub.org

The Saved Seed

Written by Brenda Moore

Illustrated by Emily Lackey

So I will be dried and stored
through weather so cold,

then gotten out in late spring
with some others I'm told.

Next the bare soil or dirt
needs to be lifted or tilled,

to prepare us for planting as
a garden they build.

They take each of us and plant
us into small holes,

and cover us with dirt and
mark our places with poles.

I'll need plenty of water
so I am hoping for rain.

If it doesn't rain often,
please use water that will drain...

...from your roof top into a
barrel or bucket below,

so that water is saved and
will continue to flow.

The sun needs to shine down
and with that water will make

a tiny plant grow out of me
since my shell has a break.

The gardener now sees me
as a plant not a seed,

My little stem is growing which
makes me proud indeed.

I have roots that grow
downward to help me get food,

from nutrients in the soil that
don't have to be chewed.

My roots also anchor me so that
I don't tip over or fall.

They help me to begin to grow
upright as I start to get tall.

Next out of the ground my
stalk grows into a vine.

I'll be growing quite fast
and looking quite fine.

Yellow flowers are starting to
grow out of my vine.

Some plants have only one flower
but I have at least nine.

Wind or insects like bees pollinate
my flowers which will mean

my flowers will become pumpkins,
but at first they'll be green.

Please help keep us healthy
by pulling out bad weeds,

and pick off bugs trying eat us
to help meet our needs.

Try not to use pesticides which can hurt an insect, bird, or worm.

The thought of poisoning my friends really makes me squirm.

The little green pumpkin will finally turn orange or yellow,

and it will grow and grow until it becomes quite a big fellow.

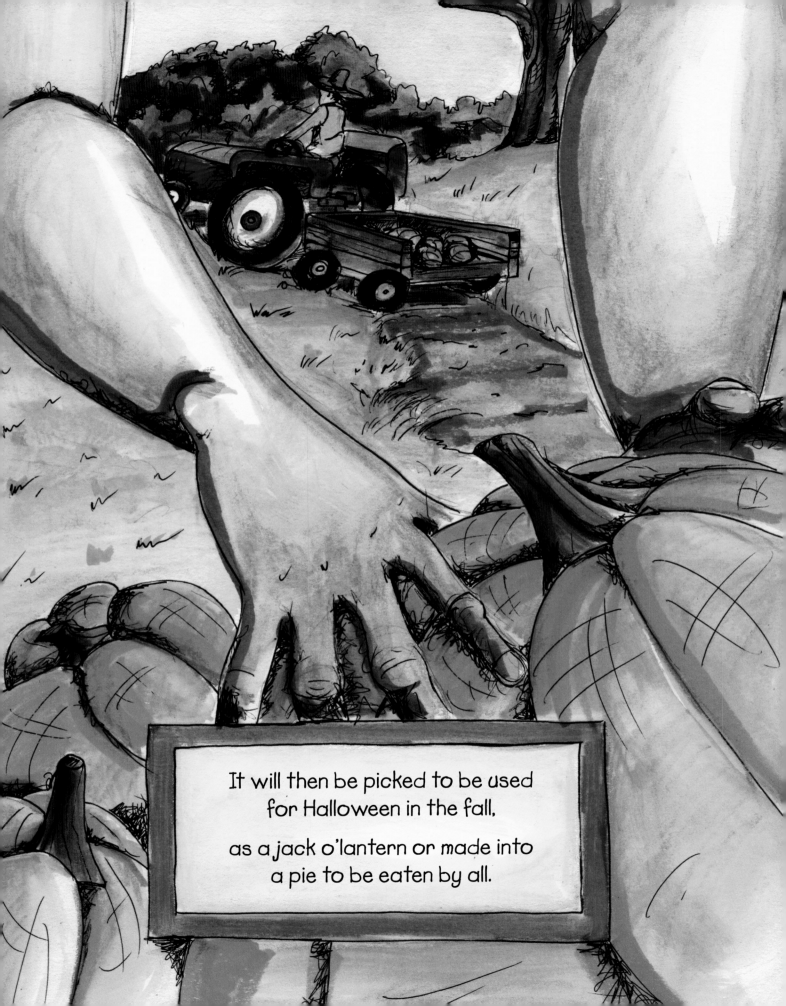

It will then be picked to be used
for Halloween in the fall,

as a jack o'lantern or made into
a pie to be eaten by all.

When you see us sold in packages
in a catalog or a store,

remember creating a seed is
really so much more

than packing us in an envelope
and putting us out to sell.

We really come from inside a fruit,
flower, cone or shell.

When Halloween pumpkins are carved,
save some seeds again,

so we can repeat this story over
and over my friend.

I'm so glad that as a saved seed
I could tell you this story

of how plants and gardens grow
to reach their full glory.

About the Author

BRENDA MOORE resides in Oak Hill, WV. She is a WVU alumnus as are her husband and children. Her husband, Ron, and she have a daughter, Rebekah, married to Andy Smith and a son, Andy, married to Emily. Her seven grandsons, Ethan, Micah, Ben, Noah, Caleb, Josh and Asher like to help her garden, as do her dogs, Brownie and Baxley. Almost everything Brenda knows about gardening she learned as a member of National Garden Clubs. She currently serves as National Garden Clubs' third vice president and is the NGC chairman of the Organizational Study committee and the Award of Excellence committee. She is the former president of West Virginia Garden Club, Inc. and is a member of the Woodland Oaks Garden Club in Oak Hill, WV. Her first book was *The Frightened Frog,* which was co-authored by Jean Ohlmann.

About the Illustrator

EMILY LACKEY grew up in Campbellsville, Kentucky. Her art career began in sixth grade when she designed t-shirts for the class. She graduated with a degree in art from Georgetown College on a tennis and art scholarship. As a mother, Emily realizes the importance of reading and outdoor connections for children. Emily lives in Chattanooga, Tennessee, with her husband, Ryan, son, Grant, and daughter, Carson.